Pax

Annie Lighthart

Pax

www.annielighthart.com

Fernwood Press
Newberg, Oregon
www.fernwoodpress.com

Cover design: Mareesa Fawver Moss

Cover painting: "Patron Saint of Turning Down the News,"
acrylic and gold leaf on wood panel, Aremy Stewart (Portland, Oregon)

Author photo: Michael Faletra

Printed in the United States of America

ISBN 978-1-59498-073-2

FOR MICHAEL AND SAM AND BENJAMIN
lux & lux & lux

&

IN MEMORY OF GORDON V. BOUDREAU
"I love the wild not less than the good."

~ Henry David Thoreau ~

Contents

*   *   *

Conditions of Happiness

Take a bed in a quiet room and wake
without pain—

a kingdom is not necessary.
Just as one bird proves flight is possible,

a crumb of bread
establishes sun and wheat,

establishes heat, attests to the presence
of a loaf and hand.

When you do not measure time,
each day is a little year,

the whole expanse in miniature,
every season

an occasion for peace.
You have what you need

is what the birds sing all morning,
and the small boat on the river

tells us again—
If there is no wind, then row.

In the Middle of Human Invention

In the middle of human invention
I took my sorry head out of its kingdom of news
and went into the sun that was the chief
of all elements. I walked warm and unthinking
through every green field. Fed as if with good
bread and wine, the hours followed and shouted.
We were a long, ridiculous, happy parade.

For once, my warring city-states slept.
For once, the workaday world lived beyond prediction.
The sun pressed its warm thumb on the earth
while I pulled my mind behind me like a red wagon
and lived a whole day without lie or desire.

Fluency

The face among the flowers was not a face but a flower
that blurred the edge of comprehension until everything
became a face, everything had eyes, everything had a mind
with secret thoughts inside, and so the barn with its smudged
windows stood aware of impatience and time, and the trowel
with its small head in the dirt plotted how not to be found,
and the old dog, who of course had her own old grey face,
came to have another one, and shifted and sighed on her rug
while thinking about philosophy and the stillness of God,
and then the depths of the afternoons she had passed alone
crossed into my heart, and the ants climbing the table stopped
and looked up, and I fell away blind into a softer knowing
as if into the flowers who took me as one of their own.

The Verge

Reason is a fine thing, but remember there are other ways
to live: by instinct or passion, or even,

maybe, by revelation. Try it. Come around again to the verge—
that place of about-to-open, near where we comprehend

and laugh and see. Why shouldn't something marvelous
happen to you? Take even an occasion like this:

a man reading at night looked up at the window to find
a moose looking in, interested and unafraid

with quiet dark eyes. He reports he has never been the same;
he finds the ungainly and miraculous everywhere.

He said it started the next night in the empty window
as he watched his reflection looking right back through.

He said he saw his own beauty, how even in his same old face
the quiet eyes were curious and ready to be true.

For the New Year

Now work: write, and make something
out of where nothing stood, or read, so that
pictures come forward, or what is still more difficult—
love, and then the nothingness makes no sound as it goes,
and the tree on the white ground begins a new branch,
though the axe and the winter considered it felled.

When We Look

When we look long at one another,
we soften, we relent, listen,

might forgive. We allow for silence
—and when we see each other,

are known, and in that moment
might change

though nothing has moved
or been spoken.

There are some who say
the walls cannot be broken,

but suddenly we are in a free place,
and the fields

that extend from its center
stretch for miles

as if out of the pupil and the iris
of that momentary kingdom.

While Reading a Russian Novel, Insects

Clearly the ants have traveled great distances, yet willingly
ascend the couch and the book. They cling to a page as it turns,
blend with the syllables of the characters' names, then fall.
They land and recover, they separate into nicknames, disperse.
The ant on my wrist confers with the ant previously on my thumb.

I sit, harming no one. I become an old city and age in patience.
New generations come, long black trains from the countryside
bringing them in. Student populations gather and disband.
Mothers, fathers, sisters arrive. They set up houses and shops,
argue in the street, cart sugar and salt from my skin.

Change is coming.
It is a flurry, a small confusion; they sense it in the air.
Soon clouds will descend like curtains of darkness.
Or darkness, like a curtain of clouds.

People and Art

People stand too close. Then they stand too far away.
They ask the wrong questions, desire to touch, disturb
the taut guards. They try to take pictures of pictures.

The lovers know it best, they who drift together from room
to room, the ones who see nothing in the museum but the
frames. Everything they see is already inside themselves:

the far ship, the resolute Madonna, the unplayed instruments,
the storm. The ruined chapel, the city in rain, the foxhounds
at rest, the back of a man. The family and possessions, the stiff
fish and flowers, and the rough little shapes of the beasts

of the field with the length of their slow going-home. They
already know the thoughts of the farmhand trailing behind,
with the wet daub of sky like a further green field. To them
the lit barn has always been ready to enter.

From its door, time is hardly more than a series of pastures
or lovely wide rooms through which the foolish keep
passing, locking each gate as they go.

To Sleep

I count on you, Sleep, thief to whom I leave open all
my belongings, for whom I unlock my door. I bless you,
and I count you among all the other good things I count,
waiting in comfortable, familiar darkness for you to arrive.
I count you again, Sleep, warm currency, you the coin
that closes eyes and then slides off with ease, you
who tips us over an unknown but wanted edge, giving an end
to the day and all we have seen. And I count and I count,
switching from blessings to sheep, who must also sleep
sometime, who must lie down in a pasture or shed
and close their strange split eyes, each marked sheep
so exhausted from bleating and grazing, none can recall
a wolf nor even how to clear a low fence. Instead
they press together, waiting to be struck down as one,
as if into the dark hold of a ship leaving at midnight
for a far better place. Now the ship moves out with the tide
and the sails are unfurled. Now the ship is a cloud,
a white flicker in the mind. Now it is you, Sleep,
and the horizon emptied of all number.

The Sixth Night of Nightmares

To make sure of you, I stand in the dark
and listen to your ragged breath,

or if you are too quiet,
kneel by your bed to check.

By now, on this sixth night of nightmares, I know
I cannot wake you, cannot speak with you,

cannot pull you out, soaked and thrashing
onto this shore. I am a useless shepherd.

But I can, if careful, lie down at the edge
of the bed by your small heap of body

until morning is the door
we both wash through.

A New Way to See Stars

They have been light and distance, and backward time—gone but still bright. They have been fixity and direction, animals, memorials, monsters, large objects, gods.

Tonight they are windows in a house set back from the road.

A man steps out with his two running dogs. Now the stars are stray sheep. They move toward the fold as he tosses white grain. Despite the bleats and the crowd, this is a feast of welcome return.

Stars fly out from the arc of his hand. They land among mouths and are eaten by day.

On Infinity

How I loved infinity as a child:
I would live forever, and so would everyone I knew,

and the house and summer, and the dog
with her certain, surely infinite bark.

How I loved every joke that circled back
to its beginning, the ones

that wore listeners right down into dirt
—exhausted, cross, and done—

while the joke went on and on
beyond sleep, beyond sky,

on with the triumph of a small rooster,
a crowing of the heart every morning of the world.

Pete and Repeat set off in a boat.
Pete fell out and who was left?

Oh, Repeat, Repeat, Repeat,
anatomy and articulation of forever and ever,

beautiful line to the only horizon,
let us sail off together with the digits of π.

Portable Typewriter on a
Small, Leaky Boat

This is the way I live, and maybe you too, if you are compelled
to write about the water and the overhanging trees,
if you keep writing sentences while the shore goes by.
Though no one is reading them, I write even more lines,
and maybe you too, switching the punctuation around
purposefully, like small fish among stones. And maybe
you trail your hand behind the boat sometimes
and then write about it while the actual hand drips
and finally dries on the keys. Is this an inexplicable life?

The people on the shore live so differently yet have an old,
familiar look. They are waving flags or maybe pages.
We can't know, you and I, because the river moves faster
even as we write it, and besides, we have only one oar.

Excessive Rumination

Yes while walking, yes while bathing, yes
while eating, surely while asleep.
Yes while driving or reading,
yes just like a cow with its huge cud,
like that, the long chew of thought,
the work of the laborious, muscular tongue.
And my god the four stomachs lugged
within me: one a leathery bag
of rationalization, the second
a sour introspective pouch,
the fretful third a chafing repetition
of the first, and the fourth
just a haversack of stew.
Miles of digestive plain—
tubes of deliberation—
the long dark tunnels of brood!
Whole days of it here, heavy
in the chair, weeks by the window,
pen in hand.
Yes like a cow
with the same dumb belch,
an occasional poem rolling between the teeth,
traveling around thick and green.

Serious Literature

The book I have never finished reading knows
I avoid it. It likes to nudge its fat spine to the edge
of the shelf, likes to consider a fall
in which it would land like a cat
if a cat were a book, which is to say, easily
and open to just the right page,

which is the page near the end I have never quite
reached, the page that will make my eyes into canyons,
that will make my mouth break from my mind
so that silently I will doubt all other truths and live
differently, or if not quite that, then live happily, stunned
as I will be by the buoyancy of time inside the stern covers
and the light pouring out on my face looking in.

Unwinter

A hundred, a thousand things on the list
and all while the day hangs outside
on a single silken thread,

and if you look up, if you go out, all
will be resolved, each salt grain dissolved,
the day given freely to every early fool
out in the yard, bare-headed, bare-footed
in the newly arrived, newly loved blur of time
in which all nouns are capsized and all requisite forms
are abandoned in this, the full tilt, first telegraphic sprint,
great god of heat, feasting fête, this good glorybody come of the sun.

Guest List

Only once, one afternoon, almost asleep on the couch,
could I come up with the perfect guests for an
imaginary dinner party—a mix of the living and dead,
the deep and the shy artfully combined with the
swashbuckling talkers. It was such a list: everyone
would say yes, and we'd sit in pairs maybe, or close
little bunches, or maybe all together at the table
while the candles burned low. Later, with a few
out on the front step, what with our immediate kinship,
the wine and warm night, I could ask them anything,
anything—historical, personal—and thus find out about life
and time. Our goodbyes would be fond and long.

But just now: no one. I can't think of a soul I'd like over,
not one for whom I'd vacuum or shove laundry
in the shower, not one for whom I'd balance fine cheese
on ridiculously small morsels of bread.

Except you, person I just saw crossing the street,
you who stopped to move a slug off the sidewalk
with a little piece of paper you took from your coat.
You, I would clean for. You, I would like to meet.

Binoculars, After All These Years

Of twiddling and sighing, of foggy
unfocusedness, of bouts with them
pressed awkwardly
like elbows in my eyes.

Lugging them, wronged by them
on mountains and oceans,
blurry infuriation, clumsy
contraptions, red rings left by them
inexplicably long
on my skin.

But now a sudden unexpected
tunneling to sight:
bird on a fencepost far across the yard—

bird seen—bird seen singing—
seen looking assiduously around, tiny bird
with three green feathers sticking up out of place,
even the spot of sun on its beak
in almost ridiculous clarity—

my two eyes blinking at it
while weeping as one—

as if coming home undeserving
after all of these years,
near-sighted and prodigal
yet welcomed and feasted,

placed at table
among the small honored guests
whose wingbeats stir
the invisible air.

The Lord Arrives Home at Daybreak

In the rough old painting at the end of the hall, the coachman
bends to set down a wooden stair. See his mouth—two colors,
two swipes of a brush—he is whistling under his breath, he is
happy. His song praises the arrival of everything, praises
the darkness from which the everything comes, welcomes
what will emerge as the fully painted day. The spotted dogs
milling around the coach are praise and the gleaming flanks
of the horses and the driver's quiet hands. And so there may be
a counterweight to destruction even in canvas and paint, praise
appearing in all corners of the frame. Like the man, the grazing
horses, the cobblestones and dogs, the world feels the sun
as good, knows the night as good, lies between them as a child
between its parents, content. Praise is the peace that rises.

Passenger

This child between us here in our dark bed asks nothing
but to be held all night, to burrow, to stay wedged
and warmed by our bodies until day.
Tomorrow he will demand more jam, will need
new shoes, will drop the toast and plate to the floor.
But just now, here, breathing softly between us,
he is a small Venetian gondolier refusing pay,
taking us back and forth all night singing
underneath the Bridge of Sighs.

House

We should be fixing it, all its parts,
siding and shingles, hinges and doors.
Between the mold and the moisture,
the whole place slides on an entropic edge
with a gradual loosening of every wedged nail.
We looked away for just a little while
—illness, the children, the world—
and never noticed the slow lines
time was pouring across the ceiling,
never saw the one winding like a root
down through the cracked floor.
Now we lean in the doorway
and look. Such work, such need.

But for tonight, you tell me, we should
close up, go to bed.
Let us leave well enough alone.
Since time takes everything equally away,
let us lay ourselves down skin to skin.
Stars are in the yard. The wet grass is singing.

The Austere Valentine You Asked For

If I could write a simple line, I would. I'd give it to you.
It would be a line as clean and pure and not as sad
as the horizon with one ship about to disappear.

People used to think you could fall off the world like that—
off the edge, all hands lost.
Some think there is no line on earth like that anymore.

I would write that line, just to see your eyes one morning
when a tiny ship reappears right there in full sail.

Angelus

Let us go to Rome and live out Roman days. In our old age
let us have a miracle in Rome. Like Elizabeth and Zacharias,
like Abraham and Sarah and every other woebegone pair,
let us conceive. Let us have a child in Rome, that scandalous
miraculous place. Let our longed-for infant be Roman born,
lusty baby rolling in warm Roman dust, lithe boy scaling
the vines of our heart, pelting a thousand Roman cats with
a thousand Roman stones.

Like good shepherds, we will shear his soft brown head,
scrub him, chide him, unlace his sandals when he sprawls out
in sleep. He will scorn subterfuge, he will rout tourists; none
but the lame, the Franciscan, and the forlorn will he favor.

Schoolboy of the Republic, alley brawler and fine citizen:
His name will be Angelo. He will grow up in Rome. On
seven hills he will lean with the putti from the holy fountains,
cheeks filled to bursting, aiming for a mark to bless.

Big Life

(ending with a line from Thomas Merton in Louisville)

Bees rose up across the field in a thrumming and undulating
alarming clump of wings. *Human,* they said
in one gold voice, *why stand so long*
without tasting? Why insist on stolen sweetness?
They hummed and swung together like beads,
then broke and spread across air. And the morning
(bodiless and bright, itself full of faceted, knowing eyes)
streamed through the day's green pulse

with everything inside it, everything in orbit, all
coming forward with Life, that enormous equable giant
strolling the streets and jumping the ponds, stirring the clouds
with a quick curious finger, seeing far, seeing all—aware,
like the bees and the morning, *there is no way of telling people*
that they are all walking around shining like the sun.

Blaze

Suddenly the peonies are too much for themselves—
heavy-headed, huge and falling—not spent, but wildly spending
utter color, unfurling perfume, sure and reckless lavish.

May I come through like this someday,
come through to a vastness on my feet and running,
the old cart of thought abandoned on the road,
and love—the heat, the secret way across the border—laying me bare.

*　　*　　*

To Be

But if it all seems ridiculous, your life just a false jewel
set in a blank expanse of space and time—
wait. There are multiple ways and winds,
cold currents, roots, vessels, eyes.
Nothing is a single, isolated story—no city,
no history, no colony, no hive.

Inside the cleft tree, hear the pervasive hum—
thousands of thousands of inhabitants
in interconnected verse, each a word on the vivified chain,
the textured elaborate swarm.
Pollen-dusted verb-body, fuzzed means, reluctant sting:
Say what you are and enter.

Ore

Not all things go by measure. In some, the alchemy's too subtle
to be weighed up, to become heft and number, to be carted out
into the light of day. Some mysteries stay as they are.

The obvious value of the lump of the heart, for example,
exists in darkness, in affection for its work.
Rooted and content in a low-roofed cave, it stays there
unrevealed. And the soul too, maybe also buried, also working,
quarrying the deep and necessary decency of the age.

And even in the middle of well-lit human invention,
the mystery of a word. *Our*, first person plural, *Our*,
deliberately said. In it, circumference. In it, no walls.
All of us within it, astounded and unburdened,
though the word sits unseen like a pebble in the soil,
nothing to catch the eye of a king.

The Lock

If you too are troubled, stuck somewhere in your life
as in a barred room at the end of a hall,

speak to the lock as if it knew you.
Chunk of metal as large as your heart,

it has passages and secrets it is wanting to tell.
A lock may rule in solitary power,

but it too can be loved.
For this very reason, jailers do not trust it.

Speak your life into its one small ear.
Trust that a word may undo you.

Let This Day

Let this day born in sackcloth and ashes
shift. Let it change, rearrange. Let it come back
made new and barking, snout pushed to table
with joy. Let it wash us wildly with its tongue
and shake its thick pelt. Let the dust rise off
in waves, in solar clouds, and let our old selves
float up in that haze, particles massed by the window,
motes among a thousand other motes. Now see
our two: we are the two motes laughing as they leave,
the two specks somersaulting right through the screen.

Of the Many Things We Are Taught

Not to eat the candy found in the road, nor the candy-shaped
rock, nor the white berries growing low in the yard next door.
Not to shout in public places: libraries, churches, airplanes,
classrooms, grocery stores, museums, government buildings,
large and echoing bathrooms or halls. Not to swallow gum nor
its wrapper, not to stick it under a chair. To sit down while eating.
To sit down while swinging. To sit down on the bus. Just to sit
down. Not to hold pins in one's mouth while sewing. Not to lick
knives. Not to wander into the street, nor dawdle at the corner.
Not to look at people frankly and say what one thinks. Not to run
out of the house with no clothes, nor, in warm rain, strip down
to the skin. Not to struggle against hats, collars, or shoes. Not to
hit or to poke. Not to approach strange dogs or squirrels or large
hissing geese. Not to half-crawl across the table to reach for the pie.
To forgive many things. To sing. To pick oneself up off the floor.

Public Singing

Sometimes, at a ballgame, many voices,
but rarely now the gathering swell and crest

of all-voice, pulse and air,
though maybe a glimpse of it in children

singing at school, standing together
in a body of sound.

Once, on a train out of the city, in flickering
underground light, a hundred strangers

in each other's arms singing "Auld Lang Syne."
Had we felt it before—

song pouring out, an instant mending,
still knowing what was bound to come

but holding and held for that one while?
Yes, once in a dark season, all of us afraid,

a voice going back and forth between us
that was neither yours nor mine.

Blackbird Tree

It is said that gods may make themselves known
in a burning bush, a cloud, or in a shower of light.

In this case, it was a blackbird in a bare winter tree.
I heard it from a block away, over traffic,

through closed windows, as if by a trick of sound.
There was a mind in that tree

as wide as anything above, and it spoke:
Everything is alright, everything is alright now.

Relief poured in—it was a feast of great peace—
nothing was lost—everything sought had been found.

It was possible to believe anything, or believe nothing
and yet stand and hear a voice in the air.

He Says I Will Kiss You Like This

And lays his eye next to mine, open,
making a new kiss, a new form, a falling into
sight, which is the beginning of all finding,
so now the two of us lay newly found and kiss
by looking, absolute in the winter-burned yard
with the yellowed scraps of moss kissing
the eye of the sun, and the mailman
with his knobbed knees kissing his route,
for in this warm wide open everything kisses
everything else and no one will look away
because how very great was the darkness before
this uptilted arriving immensity of light.

Remarkable Lives

1

There are those who have flown low over the savannah and seen
the wild-running herds and the waves of birds rising, those
who have sunk themselves into the ocean

and come up with news,
those who have seen the many cities and people
—all of us strange and new even after all of this time—

those who have heard the old songs and speech,
who live near the minarets, the mountains, the farthest
crumbling walls, the spaces

that open to wind and grasses and are complete,
and this morning in a plain yellow room,
the baby—

who took my face in his hands and looked in my eyes,
a line of light between us.

~ for Benjamin

2

The language used to describe the soul
is inadequate, the similes busy and awry.
Only the hermit knows how to speak of it, he

who has no need, he who lays out his meal
on one table. Everything in his little house is one,
one ordinary and marvelous key.

He knows there is one of everything,
that largest number, straightforward and plain.
He lays the table for a meal: one plate, one cup,

one knife, one loaf. What is God but the knife at this meal,
that which does not divide but creates singularity,
the simple crumbling continuation of the loaves of each day?

The soul is the slice lying separate and ready. Over it the voice
of the knife intones the creation: *And* and *And* and *And* and *And*.

3

I work with you, we pass on the street, I see you
in the news, or I don't see you, but know
you are there, out in the world, everywhere

on earth: you are walking, you are lifting a cup
to your lips, you are angry, you are still and soft,
and when you close your eyes, you go, as I do,

into the darkness behind them. I am thinking of you always,
thinking how we can't be known, are so afraid
and yet haven't learned how to speak.

And in all that thought, the fealty and consolation
of the human, each in our own little frame,
how necessary we are to each other,

how I might come to you and say,
My brothers and sisters—We are here! We are here! We are here!

4

I cannot do all that I would for you.
The quiet egg in the nest has more sense and purpose,
yet I keep bringing my mouthfuls of twig

and in my clumsiness don't say what I mean.
I have learned only the desire to speak, that faulty mechanism
that tends to do no good,

and at the end of the day
I go home to be struck down into sleep.
All the things of the world that are on fire with sadness

still go on burning. The embarrassment of longing
is with me at waking. Therefore let the egg
teach me silence and patience:

first the darkness, then the breaking,
then the mess of hunger-song.

5

Sometimes the world comes in too strong, like the neighbor
too long at the door, wanting a closer look—not at you
but at your life, that half-curtained glimpse.

Then it's bad news and other people's children
and lawns not kept up. It's how you shouldn't
plant those forget-me-nots out front: they'll

take over the garden, the whole street; they
are the problem, those damn weeds.
That intrusion is the price for the new screen door,

the one that lets in the air, and I say it's worth it.
You can come out again later, happy-headed and laughing.
It's a timeless world, isn't it?

The day's simple rhythm goes to its logical end.
Your weeds lift up blue stars right into evening.

6

What would change if you knew that someone was looking
for you all these years? If, on a crowded street, someone waited
for you, keeping watch everywhere for a glimpse of your face?

I don't mean a daemon or tutelary spirit, but another mystery,
more warm in its longing. And I don't know exactly the form,
if it is desire seeking you or if it is the world's great heart,

that which has lifted from all who have lived, going back
to the earliest, quietest days, that which looks for you to tell you
the news: you are forgiven, have always been forgiven,

a forgiveness as complete and kind as the air. Like air
it is all around you and lets you move freely, though you take it
for granted and give it out as speech with an unthankful mouth.

What would change if one day it found you?
What might your face look like, after?

7

Only a slight tilt makes the difference on earth—now winter,
now summer though far from the sun. And only a slight squint
of the eyes shows the wolf's teeth in harmony with the needles

of the pine. The sliding, the great slip of perception and ground!
All things come to resemble another: the heart of the worm is that
of the apple and the apple of the air that holds them,

all taking and being taken into time. And you, lifting from
yourself as surely and improbably as the flower
from the seed, you have the consolation

of being one with the human, under the minor enchantment
of our separate lives. All the things we have feared, all we have
hoped for and guessed, lead us on and yet are almost past and lost.

Is not the world in that direction? Let us tell and believe
before the strangeness of it fades.

Pax

Peace came with no words. It was a frame around darkness,
the gate to a city far in my head. It contained
murders and torture, deaths circled by fire. It held also
the husk, the green spur, and the strong second leaves. It was
a new bird, a broad field like the sea.
Peace was the shore, it was deep in the world. You were there,
we were many, there were no separate stars in that sky.

*   *   *

Octaves

Stars

Imagine the stars see clearly through the velvet length of space.
Imagine they see us running around as we do, seeming to shout
Fire! Fire! throughout the day, then strangely collapsing into
sleep each extravagant night, not waking to pull the curtains
back, hardly ever seeing how kind stars look, how their light
doesn't burn, never scorns, how across the span of a table
or over a sea of discontented talk, eyes might look at each other
that way—something, a longer question—a quiet thing arriving.

Insomnia

The sheep are native and need neither introduction nor persuasion
to enter the brain. They go over the fence and into the field as if
it had no ending, no walls, no wolves—nothing but obliging green
grass and small streams. They drift toward what they believe are
seamless rolling hills on which to graze or be alone with a flower.
At night, they watch the dome of the sky and its two glittering
stars. If there is anything else, they do not know and do not want it.
It is enough to lie down in safety and let the darkness take form.

Time

The world is not ours alone,
and to some, night is more beneficial than sun.
The river rises and they come,
the spaces between houses opening like plains.

The wave of them goes over the fence
as easily as under, though just yesterday
we thought the boards so wide and so high.
Like time, a rat squeezes, lengthens, and goes through.

Mornings to Come

Does every morning think it's the first morning,
or is each one more like the children in costume
waiting at the side of the stage—
mornings in line behind the heavy curtain,
some dreamy, some with racing hearts, one—
the morning of your death—drifting off
to look in a dim backstage mirror,
curious and forgetful of its lines and the crowd.

The Dead

Sometimes we dream of the dead so easily, so well:
the terrible knot has been won, the ribbon flows whole,
it was just a mistake, they are alive, here at the table—
they eat, they joke, they sit with a book and doze.
The world is new, everyone is here, nothing has ever
been taken. Even the night is pleasant as they turn to leave.
The dead live so close by, no one minds parting.
There is no error now. All things exchange finality for light.

How to Wake

Wake your brother with a soft voice by his pillow.
He has been very afraid.
Wake your mother with a kiss before calling her name.
Wake your grandfather with a touch on his knee, then wait—
he has far to come from the places he's been.
Wake the young dog with an open door, wake the old dog
with an outstretched hand. And yourself?
How will you wake that stubborn sleeper to life?
Look for a line let down through the water.
The silver hook is baited with a word.
Bite and awaken to that wild, clear sound.

Late

I have been late in everything—late to learn, late to wake
and to love, a belated guest at every occasion where I had meant
to come early, to see the room in full light, the faces expectant,
the first pull of sound from a quickening bow. But I have not.
I have come slowly to everything called for and now, last again,
bring my gift to a plain empty room.
                           The feast is done, but I have seen
what I've seen: this evening was a meadow made just for a slow
coming home. Someone caught a fish outside the king's palace,
and not the king nor the guards nor the gate-keeper's children
ever looked out to see. Long thought may still be rewarded
though it comes late to the hour, and a round silver mouth
caught by a fine, patient line.

Autumn

Yes, gravity wants to win, but we still live in a world
of levity—eyes opening, hope hoisting us

up from bed, bodies walking around upright—light
and lightness everywhere, every time we look—

even Keats's gnats saying so, knotting and rising
as they wail, and John in his own right, raising a fist

at the blot of death—making a life of making,
of made-things so fine that they lift

into lasting, the air around them still astonished,
still here, clear in the red balloon of lung,

lighting up our soiled tongue so that we too
float in bright listening—every cell

in concert, brain in electrical clamor, bringing into being
not heavy footfalls of the seen but buoyant

bits of mind—
breadth and depth in them, bread

and death in them, the beginning of nothing
that won't end, yet nothing

that will not also ascend,
words that fly out from the sower's bare hand.

In the Modern World

I heard today that this is the modern world,
but the world has always been modern, each era
hotly driving away from the past and in the passing
growing old while the present cruises on,
unsurprised. The moment of turning must be
a subtle, still place—slow, as if right on the head
of the pivot of time, hardly moving to the eye
as once, content not to stir, I sat on the front step
and watched my children run through the yard,
feeling just then a slip, an almost undetectable release
of forward motion. I think I grew older, old-fashioned,
the peace of it slow honey slow on the tongue.

A Great Wild Goodness

One morning I was looking out the window
when a great wildness came over me:
I wanted to be kind to everything. I promised
not to kill the spider on the wall; in the cold
I took the dog for the long walk she'd been wanting;
I fetched a trashcan lid for an ornery neighbor
and did not, just then, add a single adjective to his name.
I went back inside to the laundry and dishes
with a clean heart such as I have never had.

Before dinner the wild goodness bellowed *Too tame!*
Too tame! so I went outside without my coat
and shouted poems up the alleys
until my children came home with their small,
warm hands. Then we ate bread
in the kitchen, unafraid to be happy.
The stars in wild darkness were right over our heads.

Blessings on the Rat

Blessings even on the rat in this provincial station
where no hours come except to quickly leave
so that the stationmaster grieves undisturbed
while the tracks continue unabated,
and domestic peace is had solely by the rats
behind the boards, the little ones blind
in bare-skinned sleep.

The only dead one is away by the barn,
splayed in the rain like a cuneiform letter
that no one passing will ever see
or poke with a stick or bother to stoop down to read.

Diogenes

Having a philosopher for a neighbor is much like having
an old horse next door: it's a beautiful sight in the morning
to see him stand and think under the misty trees, and sometimes
he'll let you open the gate and come close. But on other days,
he bites. One must always walk a wide circle behind him.
A kick at the head leaves thoughts that linger and bruise.

When struck, you go home knowing that you too will die
and that the pasture fence you firmly put in, the posts
you sank so deeply, already lean and groan. In the kitchen,
the water works itself up to a good steam, pots rattle, the bread
rises right. Nothing but you has changed. Out the window
your neighbor potters in his garden, digs a few onions.
When he thinks you aren't looking, he leans over the fence, picks
your last apple. His bite is enormous. You can hear it all day.

The Night Is Large

It is good to be occupied and have something to do after dinner, and you have a thick book here, balanced heavily on the arm of the chair, ready to read or ready to fall. It has waited for years. Once, cornered at a party, you claimed to have read it. Sometimes you think you have. Didn't you take a required class that discussed it? Didn't you pass an exam in which it weighed mightily? Don't you, even now, touching its serious cover, understand your life's fear in a whole new way? The night outside the room is large. It is as large as the sea. The last snowy hill is a white leviathan bent on destruction, and the moon is a lidless eye.

In the Evening I Read
a Poem to the Dog

There are other lonelinesses than ours, but tonight
ours has the texture and depth of an old stubbled field.
We are rich with it but a little sorry for ourselves
and so we sit on the front step as on a desolate shore,
not restless or waiting for anyone.
Because the dog's chief affection is not for me,
she gives my poem a fair hearing. By the seventh line
she closes her eyes and runs into dream.
It is not insult. We have come to this particular night
through the doorway of many others, knowing now
that sleep and language are likely to ferry us through.
Though the dream takes her to the coast where she ran
when young, her face looks older, more grey than I've seen.
I leave off the poem. She moans and chases the infinite gulls.

Time Is Doing Something to Us

Time is doing something to us so gradually and softly
we don't notice for years,

and then the work is done—
we are older.

A craftsman who works this slowly
is a master,

and it seems unwise
to challenge that art.

Then what?
Then feel the morning air. Walk out at night

as if into the sky.
It is just a little while after all.

The tree you are under will tell you
it moved into time and grew deeper.

We too can do this.
The master leaves a mystery

that breaks out once in leaf, once
in clarifying fire.

One of the Rules of Stories

The fairy godmothers who bring blessings to the child
cannot undo the curse of the one
who gave the gift of harm.
But we are to keep in mind the proper order of the tale:
the curse is given before the last good godmother
bends over the cradle, and so what cannot be undone
can at least be tempered,
or encompassed in a kinder hand.

In such a way, during the terrible years,
my father gave me, his strange youngest,
books to read alone in my room,
saying *Good things often come late and small,*
meaning his gift and my life at the same quiet time.

Scraps of Paper

The crumpled one wedged at the bottom of the stair,
the you of years ago insisting this list must be done.

The one ripped from a notebook and mistakenly left on the
windshield for someone else, a loved stranger with flowers
sketched through her name.

A turquoise one blown into the yard, naming Charlemagne
and half the kings of old France.
(Which of the taciturn neighbors contemplates such things?)

And Pascal's folded God-note, written out twice, sewn
into his coat, found after he died:
From about half-past ten in the evening until about half-past
midnight.
Certitude, certitude, feeling, joy, peace.
Eternally in bliss, in exchange for a day of hard training
in this world.
May I never forget your words.

Scrap kept close,
words firmly stitched in.

Prayer to Patrick Kavanagh

Come grub with me, Old Man,
here in this makeshift garden,

muddy and foolishly at work
where all is still dearth and hunger,

one hand in the sod reaching around,
the Lord of the place

quick-dodging our pinch and grasp.
Or pull me up out of the thing altogether—

rooty, mandrake, bawling.
Take me with you walking.

For that one unfettered while
I would be earthed matter without quarrel,

a small dry cut
out of God's well-flooded field.

Hay

There were no machines on that farm. We were young,
we raked hay by hand. We shoveled, forked, piled.
Golden with grit, we became hay men and women, bits
in our eyes, hay sifted into collars and boots. At noon we
lay stunned in a half-done stack until shouted back to the
work. We pitched higher and faster until each shape was
thatched and thick. Then in darkness, when the rain came
hard, we shucked off our clothes and washed by the trough.
The old farmer stumped away to the barn, pleased at the
crop, how the outer hay kept the inner hay dry. Out in the
yard, inside our wet skin, every thought tasted like fire.

Word from the Farm

It's likely you'll die, just as it's likely
you'll be a little happy and a little sad
between this point and then,

but maybe all the days won't be duels
in which you are worsted.
It's likely that the work you do

and the work you love
may be entirely separate elements,
but if for a while they live together

then in the end when the fires burn
you're likely to remember a clearing of skies,
how there were days so sure of purpose

your heart took every fence cleanly
without looking down.

Companion

The body keeps us ordinary. It says *Sleep*, and we must,
it says *Eat*, and we do. It says *I grow old*,

and we understand it to mean *We grow old*:
the voice in the mind and the head that shelters it

in the echoing chamber. But the body will not admit
the two as separate, though it converses,

though it clearly speaks, to another.
It believes in the brain,

both mass and thought contained together,
electric currents and substance housed

as one and set on its shelf
of white bone. The body does not listen

to the mind's long protestations
and grief. It takes us home at night

to undress and lie down.
It says *Be at peace*. It says *Hold still*.

It says *I know to what end I am going*.
The body understands that when you lean your head

in your hands, you feel the weight of the one self
heavily moving forward in time. That is when it says

Look, it is morning—
although a bit more softly, before making you rise.

Botanic Garden

We crossed an ocean before you first saw your soul,
and in an older country were given it in a garden—

beautiful flame of the small fox you knew as your very self.
And why would the soul not dart out and stop

at the sight of you? We are always walking toward each other,
though we forget every waking.

From the gate, I saw only your stilled head and opened hands,
heard only the bells of the city call the air,

and yet it suddenly seemed that we come into love
from little distances—the eyes with their clasp of seeing,

the in-breath before comprehension.
And so in radiance as in love, the garden lit all things at once:

a deep bell rang in the trees, and another answered
from a farther field,

you and a fox stood in stillness, center
of all centers, struck sparks rising and falling.

Fragile Craft

See how the sidewalk does not attempt to be
a boulevard. Be like that—a stretch of plain self
from door to street. Be the ant
moving toward a crumb on the plate,
one of many climbing enormity.

Haven't you had enough of the thin film of disguise,
the dodge, the fever of persisting in
what is not quite true—
some better, other self?

Culprit of your own life, try a true name.
Call yourself *Love*, call yourself *Dear One*.
Put an arm around your shoulders and go home
for soup and crackers and a glass of ginger ale.

In the morning the fever might be gone,
burned up in one clean honest sleep.
The hand on your forehead could be your own,
as well as the physician's pronouncement:

Fragilis ratis: the fragile craft:
mortal but still able to rise.

Bound

In the safety pin comes the difference
between time and eternity—mouth paused
open to air, mouth closed inside the
long loop—an eye at either end,

watching. And in the middle,
pressure, indecision, a tight scissoring
of position, the slight chance to
make things right—a little brightness
of motion, a moment before the impulse
of prayer is lost in the ornament of prayer,
a hardly perceptible shaking in the jaw
as it hovers between taking in
awe and breathing out fear.

And in there too, the sight, the glint
of the fine silver pin, the point now near
now far, now beauty now pain,
with necessity asking again and again,
Aren't you already hinged like a shadow
to both darkness and light?
So why not be pinned to God
though pinned to earth, no longer a jabbering
cub playing at isolation, but a soul
riding a steeled point bound for completion—

about to be, in the process of, already begun,
secured to the firmament, the charged,
the atom, the garment, your hand a small hand
at the blazing edge of that hem.

To My Soul

after Hadrian

The day you turned toward me laughing
I saw that you were strange and beautiful
and already running away

Lamb and Lion

Will there be a time when the seen and unseen
lie down together

like lamb and lion, like skin
along skin, the warmth between them

rising from the far older world
we do not know—the place that is

within this one, as a walled garden
is within the city and yet unknown

even to those who try the locked gate.
And will it be morning

when everything changes, or does revelation
need night to temper its force

so that we step into knowledge
feeling only dark water,

hardly aware of the horizon
playing out beyond our hands.

> (I see that I have been asking questions
> while withholding the mark
> that would leave them dangling alone on their hook.)

> (Again I choose the little pebble
> to set against the great closed door.)

Ghost

I
In the dull, careless years when I believed
that the separate shouts of the living and the dead

remained on each side of the boundary of fire,
I couldn't see that the world resists division,

that even in this it is always
both wedding and funeral, an invisible procession

winding through every street—every life bound
tight to the rest and lit

even as it is extinguished. And while I stammered
and insisted that nothing could be salvaged

past death's clean line, the world went right on
joining the pieces and playing back every voice,

which is to say making a music that carries,
a truth I would have thought absurd if I didn't now

hunger for it so fiercely, if my mouth
had not acknowledged that it still speaks to you,

or that I have heard your voice twice now from the trees
and go there to hunt it down in my own haunted woods.

II

While listening to birds
I asked about death.

What is it if not this—
a call toward, a call to,
a call—

at the edge of the green branch
three knowings in the bird.

The last not a song
but an urge and direction—

to go—
to fall into air.

III

This was your kindness, you who were hardly here,
a thought without speech, an idea of a gaze:

you gave me back to myself, warmer, more
human, in a body hinged to earth.

Now I know what it is to draw breath,
to be in skin, to carry voice

through muscle and bone. And the human language,
I feel it everywhere in me, easy,

tongue and ear, the desire to be understood,
to lay down fingerprints of words.

But now you are leaving. The entire night is outside the walls,
and you riding past.

To the Language

I am in love with you. You are the handprints on the glass
to which I fit my own, the cup I drink from
and also what fills it, and also still the emptiness left.
You, the bed and remembered night.

You take nothing for yourself.
You tell me that stones on a mountain allow travelers to stop
and look out, having no need to see for themselves,
being satisfied, being stone, what is willing to hold.

I begin to understand.
But when the mountain is alone again,
and while the broken grasses mend
around each footprint, the wind comes
to speak with the stones.

Like that, Words, I would speak with you.
Like that, my breath on each small rough face.

Lantern

Some evening, almost accidentally, you might yet understand
that you belong, are meant to be, are sheltered—

still foolish, but looking out the door with a contented heart.
This is what the king wants and the old man and woman

and even the busy young if they knew, and you have it
by no grace of your own, standing in the doorway

with loose empty hands. Now your heart lights your mind,
a little lantern bobbing within you,

giving out not thought or feeling but confluence,
something else. On what do you pour out this light?

The wet street is empty, one wren in the yard. Let us
redefine love and wreckage, time and weeds.

Pour out your lantern light on the grass, on the bird,
great and small worlds. Don't go inside for a long, long time.

Acknowledgments

Grateful acknowledgment is made to the publications in which these poems first appeared:

"A Great Wild Goodness": *Poems in the Waiting Room*; "Blaze": *Poems from the Garden: The Poeming Pigeon*; "Companion": *Hunger Mountain*; "Conditions of Happiness": *Come Shining: Essays and Poems on Writing in a Dark Time*; "Fluency": *Miramar Review*; "For the New Year": *Floating Bridge Review*; "Hay": *Carve*; "A New Way to See Stars": *Prairie Wolf Review*; "The Night Is Large": *Carve*; "Octaves": *Inflectionist Review*; "Of the Many Things We Are Taught": *Serving House Journal*; "Peace": *New Madrid Review*; "Portable Typewriter on a Small, Leaky Boat": *Timberline Review*; "Public Singing": *Iron Horse Review*; "Remarkable Lives 1": *All We Can Hold: Poems of Motherhood*; "To Be": *Poems-for-All*; "The Verge": *Kosmos Quarterly*; "When We Look": *New Madrid Review*; "While Reading a Russian Novel, Insects": *Inflectionist Review*.

"Big Life": Excerpt from *Conjectures of a Guilty Bystander* by Thomas Merton. Reprinted with permission of Penguin Random House.

A number of poems from *Pax* were included in *Lantern*, which won the 2017 Wells College Press Chapbook Award. With thanks to Rich Kegler, Dan Rosenberg, and Wells College Press for their love of books.

"To Be" was published as a tiny beautiful book by Richard Robert Hansen in his *Poems-for-All* series. His mission to scatter poems like seeds throughout the world is a tremendous gift.

With thanks to New Zealand's *Poems in the Waiting Room* for publishing "A Great Wild Goodness" and sending out eight thousand poetry cards to hospices, nursing homes, prisons, and medical clinics. Their tireless work for healing is a kindness beyond measure.

Many thanks to Eric Muhr and Fernwood Press for giving this book a home.

Biography

Annie Lighthart started writing poetry after her first visit to an Oregon old-growth forest. She has taught at Boston College and with writers of all ages, teaching poetry workshops wherever she can. Poems from her books *Iron String* and *Lantern* have been featured on *The Writer's Almanac* and in various anthologies, including *Poetry of Presence: An Anthology of Mindfulness Poems* and *Healing the Divide*. Annie's poems have been turned into choral music, used in healing projects in Ireland, England, and New Zealand, and have traveled farther than she has.